Your Passport To Fun & Flavor

ISBN 978-0-615-84500-5

Cover, book design and creative direction by Carrie Creegan, Ideaworks Food Marketing

Food photography by Maria Scott Studios.
mariascottphotos.com
maria@mariascottphotos.com
570.262.5118

Remmi Photography by Lasting Impression Photography
www.liphotography.com
Info@liphotography.com
918-622-7868

Additional photography by:
Royal Studios
Blue House Media
Metro Appliances and More
Nicollette Smith

Food styling by Peggy Hansbury.

Global Cooking for Kids: Your Passport to Fun & Flavor is available at special discounts when purchased in bulk for premiums and sales promotions, as well as for fund-raising or educational use. Special editions or book excerpts can also be created to specifications. For details, contact Ideaworks Food Marketing at the address below, or send an e-mail to info@ideaworksfoodmarketing.com.

Ideaworks Food Marketing
301 West Main Street
Plymouth, PA 18651
www.ideaworksfoodmarketing.com

Printed in the United States

First printing May 2013

GLOBAL COOKING for kids

Hi! I'm Remmi. Thank you for being interested in cooking, and thank you for buying my book. I am all about healthy eating and kids having fun in the kitchen. Writing this book was a really big adventure for me. I'm hoping it will be an adventure for you. You can explore the world through food. I want to inspire you to get in the kitchen and have some fun, cook healthy and enjoy life and the love of food. I've always wanted to be a cook star, and you can be a cook star, too!

xoxo
Remmi

ABOUT ME

HISTORY I am 12 years old, I am the sixth of seven children and I am from Oklahoma. I was adopted from China when I was ten months old, and my Chinese name is Yang Fu Shun. I love everything about food; eating is the best part. You already know I love to learn about food and food history. I started in the kitchen when I was four. My mom put me to work washing vegetables and making salads. When I was seven, I started to make full meals by myself. At age nine, I started my first web series: "Cook Time with Remmi™." My brother, Abe, gave mom and me the idea to do the series.

COOK TIME WITH REMMI™ What got us thinking about the show was concern about the childhood obesity epidemic. At the time, Oklahoma was one of the top states with a high obesity rate. After a lot of research, we realized there is a lot of good information out there for kids and families. What we didn't see was a strong tie-in to improved nutrition through learning how to cook. The show was our creative way to link the skill of cooking to improved nutrition. Our objective was to get kids in the kitchen while having fun, too!

AMAZING OPPORTUNITIES Once the show started to air on my website, I started to get a lot of attention both locally and nationally. Within a year, I was named Amazing Kid of the Month; I was selected as one of seven kids from across the county as a "Rock Star" Learner by Apple; named a "Super Star" for the Ask, Listen, Learn Team and, soon after, named "Top 20 to Watch" by The Century Council. Through this award specifically, I got to meet Olympians, elite athletes and top business leaders—crazy, huh?

PARTNERSHIPS My second series started soon after when we created a partnership with Oklahoma State University Institute of Technology Culinary Arts Program. In each episode of the series, in the first half of the show, I traveled to different chefs' kitchens to learn a new cooking technique. In the second half of the show, I prepared a meal using the learned technique and presented it to the teaching chef. This series aired on Cox TV in Oklahoma. It was a time when a lot was happening-filming with a professional production company, learning true cooking techniques, meeting objectives of our partners and sponsors and, most importantly, not disappointing the chefs who taught me. I was constantly creating, testing and re-testing new recipes just about every day of the week!

PROMOTING HEALTH This past year I had the honor of being named the "Student Ambassador for Health and Nutrition" by Sodexo for all of North America. Through this, I have the opportunity to work with their Executive Chefs in over 500 school districts, and I represent over 3 million students. My recipes are served in all of their cafeterias. Through this partnership, I have had great opportunities to travel all over the country and appear in national venues, both with adults and children, doing what I love to do: cooking and promoting healthy eating.

I think of the kitchen as a science lab, a place to experiment. What's cool is that you get to eat the experiment!

Global Cooking

When I got lucky enough to be asked to write a cookbook, my publisher presented me with some ideas and themes for the book. I instantly knew I wanted to write this one. I knew it would be the hardest one to write. I love food, and I love food history. It's the history that makes food interesting. In the book, I selected one country from each of the seven continents. Narrowing down which countries I was going to write about was the most difficult part of the book, but it was a fun process, because I got to capture a new vision of the world, from a culinary perspective and gained a broader understanding of cultures through food.

Recipe Selection

When selecting the recipes, I tried to pick popular dishes and ingredients that are served and available in that country. For the dishes, I was inspired to experiment, I read A LOT of recipes for the same dish before I began. My approach to writing a recipe is to always use a lot of vegetables (fortunately there is only one vegetable I am not crazy about), add natural sweetness through the use of fruits (we kids like our sweets), go light on spices (making it easier for kids to try new foods), minimize ingredients and steps (making it easier for kids to tackle), substitute low-fat ingredients (the results are amazing), present some fun facts or history (that is what makes food interesting) and present the dish beautifully (Chef Minden taught me we eat with our eyes). I also select economical foods, so my recipes are budget-friendly, too!

Complete Menus

Each country has a complete menu from appetizers all the way to desserts. If you prepare the entire menu, you would be making a feast, which is cool. But, you can still create a satisfying meal just by fixing two or three of the menu items. Each of my recipes will serve four really hearty appetites. Use my book as a guide. Change the recipes, create your own, explore foods from other countries and make food fun for YOU!

How To Use This Book

Use this book as a map to guide you through the fun and delicious sides of some of the world's most interesting countries! Every country's section will have tips from me about the dishes we're creating, along with brain teasers and fun facts. Test your knowledge of all these exotic places we're "traveling" to. Take notes in the Recipe Notes section of what you made, who helped you cook and all the great memories you create, so you can remember the great time you had preparing these dishes! The "Map It" feature at the beginning of each section gives you a letter and number so you can pinpoint just where these tasty treats are coming from on the map in the back of the book.

BRAIN TEASERS

CHEF REMMI TIP

FUN FACTS

Sources:
"Morocco." - Wikitravel. <www. wikitravel.org/en/Morocco/>. Harned, Cathy. "Moroccan Bread Information." Astray Recipes. 24 Sept. 1994. < http://www.astray.com/recipes/?show=Moroccan%20bread%20information/>. "The Legend of the Sapo - La Leyenda Del Sapo!" The Story of the Frog Game or Juego De Sapo. 2010. < http://www. zappogame.com/th.html/>. "Discover Lebanon Tourism Guide, Maps, Forum Chat, Weather." Discover Lebanon Tourism Guide, Maps, Forum Chat, Weather. < www.discoverlebanon.com/>. "Countries and Their Cultures." Lebanese. < http://www.everyculture.com/wc/Japan-to-Mali/Lebanese.html/#bPage/>. Hughes, Zora. "Beef and Potato Saute inspired by "Potato Fry" in Taste of Lebanon". "Italian Culture & Heritage Activities for Children." Global Post. <http://everydaylife.globalpost.com/italian-culture-heritage-activities-children-7266.html/>. "Baby Names with Meaning Around The World." Baby Name Meanings, Meaning of Names Boys and Girls. <http://www.babynology. com/>. "The Best Cuisine on Antarctic Ice." Scientist at Work The Best Cuisine on Antarctic Ice Comments. <http:// scientistatwork.blogs.nytimes.com/2012/08/23/the-best-cuisine-on-antarctic-ice/>.

TO THOSE WHO HELPED ME GET HERE

My Start
Brenda Butchee, **Ed Wampler** and the **Cook Time Team**.

My Jump to the Next Level
Blue House Media – Thank you for the very creative series and believing in me.

My Incredible Sponsors and Partners
Oklahoma State University Institute of Technology Culinary Arts Program
Thermador
Rick Federico
Metro Appliances and More
Linda Johnson
Whole Foods Market

Lorah Gerald
Shad Benoit
Steve Cramer
Sodexo
Richard Hill
Corbin Anderson

My Inspiring Instructors
Chef Avona
Chef Colby
Chef Fusco
Chef Gitschner
Chef Harp

Chef Harris
Chef Jungo
Chef Marlow
Chef Minden
Chef Richards

Chef Schlossberg
Chef Van Glabbeek
Chef Werry

My Fabulous Support Team
Ideaworks – who inspired me to write this book; **Libby Bonbright**, a true angel; **Royal Studios** for my wonderful new series; my photographer **Denice Toombs** – your work is fabulous; my manager, the amazing **Lauren Lloyd**; my awesome family; and especially my partner – my mother, **Nancy**.

And another BIG Thank You to **Whole Foods Market** for providing the
healthy and beautiful foods for my endless recipe testing, my series and my book.

I THANK YOU, AND I LOVE YOU!

Remmi Smith

TABLE OF contents

AFRICA

MOROCCO

The country of Morocco is located in the Northwest region of Africa. Moroccan cuisine has many influences, including African, Spanish and European, with a heavy focus on Mediterranean-style foods. This exotic place is filled with delicious sights and even more delicious foods!

Chef Remmi Smith
Map It
★ C2
Global Cooking

MENU

Moroccan Meatball Tagine
Lemon Couscous with Minted Yogurt Sauce
Pita Salad
Fresh Oranges with Cinnamon

MOROCCAN
Meatball Tagine

INGREDIENTS

THE TAGINE

1 T olive oil
1 large onion (medium dice)
3 garlic cloves (whole)
¾ c celery (large dice)
3 ½ c carrots (cut in 2" lengths)
2 c vegetable broth
1 (28) oz can diced tomatoes with juice
½ t cinnamon
1 t turmeric
1/2 t saffron
3 T fresh cilantro (1 T reserved for garnish)
2 T fresh parsley
Salt and pepper to taste
3 c fresh spinach

MEATBALLS

2 lb ground beef
½ c panko bread crumbs
2 eggs
1/3 c chopped onion
1/3 c chopped cilantro
½ t cumin
½ t ground nutmeg
½ t ground cinnamon
Salt and pepper to taste

DIRECTIONS

MEATBALLS:

In a large bowl, mix all of the ingredients together and then form into 2-inch meatballs. Set aside.

THE TAGINE

In a large pot that can go in the oven, sauté the onions, celery and garlic in oil for two minutes. Add all of the remaining ingredients except for the spinach and bring to a boil on top of the stove.

Turn the stove off and gently place the meatballs in the stew. The meatballs should be covered by the liquid. Place a lid on the pot and place in preheated 350-degree oven for 45 minutes. Take tagine out of the oven and gently stir the fresh spinach into the stew. Place lid back on pot and let it sit for 10 minutes.

To serve, place lemon couscous in medium bowl. Top with a serving of the tagine and a heaping spoonful of the minted yogurt sauce.

Tangines are slow cooked and the possibilities of bringing different ingredients together are endless. I love this one the most because of the meatballs – I mean, what kid doesn't love meatballs?! -Remmi

My Recipe Notes

Entries Entrées / Entradas	Visas	Departures Sorties / Salidas

Age:

Date:

Where I cooked:

Entries Entrées / Entradas	Visas	Departures Sorties / Salidas

Who I cooked for/with:

This recipe is:

Other:

 BRAIN TEASERS

I am Bugs Bunny, and I am the capital of Morocco.

I am a country on a different continent, I rhyme with rain and I am 9 miles north of Morocco.

CHEF REMMI TIP

Morocco is well-known for their fabulous cuisine. While this menu has some of my favorites, there are so many other great dishes to try. Also experiment with this tagine and use lemons, olives or raisins to change up the flavor of this dish.

Saffron is an expensive spice, but you really do not have to use a lot in a dish. The money is worth it. The flavor is sublime!

Saffron, a spice which comes from the Saffron Crocus flower

Black Olives

FUN FACTS ABOUT MOROCCO

Spices are very important to Moroccan cooking and chefs and cooks create their own "Ras el hanout," meaning "the head of the shop," – a mixture of 20 to 40 different spices.

Taliouine is the "Saffron Capital," and it is known to produce high quality saffron.

Lemon Couscous
WITH MINTED YOGURT SAUCE

INGREDIENTS

2 c water
1 t olive oil
2 T lemon juice
2 c couscous
Salt and pepper to taste
¼ t lemon zest

DIRECTIONS

In medium pan, bring water to boil. Add oil, lemon juice, couscous, salt and pepper. Place a lid on the pan and turn heat off. Let sit for 5 minutes. Add the lemon zest and fluff couscous with fork.

Hey, I really wanted to make lemon rice, which is so great, but couscous is the National Dish. Try it! I really loved it when I made it.

Serve with Minted Yogurt Sauce recipe.
Yogurt…need I say more? You know I love yogurt!

My Recipe Notes

Entries Entrées / Entradas **Visas**		Departures Sorties / Salidas
Age:		
Date:		
Where I cooked:		

Entries Entrées / Entradas **Visas**		Departures Sorties / Salidas
Who I cooked for/with:		
This recipe is:		
Other:		

 # BRAIN TEASER

I am never wrong, I have two of them and I use this to eat with in Morocco.

Couscous is the national dish, and this one is fairly simple. Do some experimenting with adding vegetables and different spices.

Couscous

Fresh veggies

FUN FACTS ABOUT
FACT MOROCCO

Moroccans are big on hospitality, and they love to prepare and cook big meals. They believe foods cooked in the home are much better and many never eat at restaurants.

Ghazaouet
Tlemcen

juig

Minted Yogurt SAUCE

INGREDIENTS

1 ½ c plain yogurt
½ c cucumber
1 T dried mint
Pepper to taste .

DIRECTIONS

In small bowl, combine all ingredients.

Serve with the Lemon couscous!

My Recipe Notes

Entries
Entrées / Entradas **Visas** Departures
Sorties / Salidas

Age:

Date:

Where I cooked:

Entries
Entrées / Entradas **Visas** Departures
Sorties / Salidas

Who I cooked for/with:

This recipe is:

Other:

BRAIN TEASERS

I love this when
I sleep, and I am
what you sit on
when eating a meal.

Answer: Pillow

Remmi munches on some
traditional Moroccan cuisine.

CHEF REMMI TIP

Moroccans use all types of meats to make a tagine. Try chicken for a low fat and economical tagine. Also, you can make a vegetable tagine using squash with white beans for a meatless meal.

Remmi and her friends play a game of "cache cache"

FUN FACTS ABOUT
MOROCCO

FACT

Children love to play "cache cache". It is a game of hide-and-seek.

Elders are very respected in this society and have a lot of influence on the family.

Pita Salad

INGREDIENTS

SALAD
3 c Romaine lettuce (sliced)
¼ c tomato (small dice)
½ c cucumber (small dice)
4 pita breads

DRESSING
½ c olive oil (or safflower oil-it's lighter!)
¼ c Lemon juice
2 garlic cloves (minced)
3 T dried mint
Salt and pepper to taste

DIRECTIONS

Prepare ingredients as directed. Place lettuce, tomato and cucumber in medium bowl. Place pita on baking sheet and warm in 400-degree oven. In small bowl or jar, add dressing ingredients and mix. Toss salad with dressing (may not need all of the dressing). Cut warmed pitas in half and stuff with salad.

I have made pita salad forever. To make this Moroccan, I added the tomatoes and cucumbers. I usually make it simple with just the lettuce and the dressing. It is the only salad my sister, Elizah, will eat. Totally simple and totally the best. Make sure you have enough for seconds!
- Remmi

My Recipe Notes

Entries / Entrées / Entradas	Visas	Departures / Sorties / Salidas
Age:		
Date:		
Where I cooked:		

Entries / Entrées / Entradas	Visas	Departures / Sorties / Salidas
Who I cooked for/with:		
This recipe is:		
Other:		

 # BRAIN TEASERS

In the city of Chefchaouen there is a tradition of painting all houses this color, and I am this when I am sad.

I am a collection of maps, I am really tall and I separate the coastline from the Sahara Desert.

Answers:
Blue
Atlas Mountains

Homemade "batbout," or pita

🗒️ CHEF REMMI TIP

Find a recipe to make "batbout," which is similar to pita bread. It is not too hard to make, and it is really delicious!

Once you try the salad-stuffed pita, you are going to be hooked on this, I promise!

FUN FACTS ABOUT
MOROCCO

Households make their own bread every day, and after it is shaped they make their family mark on it. The children then take it to the local bakery to be baked.

fresh oranges
WITH CINNAMON

INGREDIENTS

2 oranges (sliced in ½-inch rounds)
¼ t cinnamon

DIRECTIONS

Prepare oranges as directed. Place on medium
plate and sprinkle with cinnamon.

Moroccans serve fruit
at the end of a meal.
This is so simple and
delicious!

My Recipe Notes

Entries Entrées / Entradas	Visas	Departures Sorties / Salidas

Age:

Date:

Where I cooked:

Entries Entrées / Entradas	Visas	Departures Sorties / Salidas

Who I cooked for/with:

This recipe is:

Other:

 BRAIN TEASER

It is my official name as a country, because I am ruled by a King and I am a magical Disney park.

Morocco coastline on the Mediterranean Sea

Answer:
Kingdom

CHEF REMMI TIP

When serving fruit as a dessert, try different spices to jazz it up; like ginger, nutmeg and anise. Be careful not to use too much!

Dried oranges, spices and nuts

FUN FACTS ABOUT
FACT
MOROCCO

Morocco is located on the second largest continent, Africa.

Morocco is located in the Northwestern corner of Africa and it has two bodies of water on its border, the North Atlantic Ocean and the Mediterranean Sea.

AUSTRALIA

Australia is located Southeast of Asia, in the middle of the Pacific Ocean. Australian food is influenced by the outdoor-focused people of its country. Many foods come directly from the land and are main ingredients in many dishes. Australia is a great collection of people and flavors!

MENU

Lemony Smashed Potatoes
Salad with Butternut Squash
Cottage Pie
Fruit Salad

Map It
★ H5

Lemony Smashed
POTATOES

INGREDIENTS

12 new potatoes (small)
2 T olive oil
1½ T lemon juice
¼ c fresh parsley (sliced)
1 c sour cream (nonfat)
1½ T chives (chopped small)
Sea salt and pepper

DIRECTIONS

Boil potatoes in pot of water until tender then drain. On a large baking sheet, oil the pan with ½ T of the olive oil. Place the potatoes on the baking sheet.

Smash each potato with your hand until they slightly break open. Mix the remaining oil with the lemon juice. Drizzle mixture over the potatoes. Salt and pepper the potatoes. Bake in 450 degree oven for 25 minutes or until the potatoes are a bit crispy and golden. Remove potatoes from baking sheet with a spatula and stack them, like a pyramid, on a medium plate. Sprinkle with the parsley. Mix the chives with the sour cream and serve on the side.

This is a great appetizer,
and it is unbelievably delicious!

The Great Barrier Reef

FACT FUN FACTS ABOUT AUSTRALIA

Australia is the smallest of the 7 continents and is surrounded by 2 oceans and 3 seas.

The Great Barrier Reef is located off the coast of Queensland in the Coral Sea and is the largest reef in the world.

 BRAIN TEASERS

I have the longest and straightest railroad track in the world, I am home to mining but not a lot of people, I am a large desert and I am the opposite of in and the opposite of front.

There are more than 10,000 of me, I surround Australia, I am always near water, I am patrolled by "lifesavers" and kids love to build sandcastles on me.

The Australian Outback

Answers:
Outback
Beaches

TIP CHEF REMMI TIP

I LOVE smashed potatoes! I have made these many times but did not know that they are an Australian dish. These are awesome, awesome, awesome!

My Recipe Notes

Entries
Entrées / Entradas **Visas** Departures
Sorties / Salidas

Age:

Date:

Where I cooked:

Entries
Entrées / Entradas **Visas** Departures
Sorties / Salidas

Who I cooked for/with:

This recipe is:

Other:

Salad
WITH BUTTERNUT SQUASH

INGREDIENTS

3 c baby spinach
2 c Romaine lettuce (sliced 1" pieces)
1 T olive oil
2 c butternut squash (1" cubes)
8 strawberries (sliced)
1/4 c pomegranate seeds
1/4 c green onions (sliced)
1/4 c almonds (sliced/toasted)
1 T fresh parsley (sliced)
Salt and pepper to taste
¼ c olive oil
2 T red wine vinegar

DIRECTIONS

Preheat oven to 400 degrees. Prepare squash and place on cookie sheet. Drizzle with oil and salt and pepper. Bake for 15 minutes or until tender.

Prepare all ingredients as directed.

Place lettuce on platter. Layer remaining ingredients in order listed. Mix oil and red wine vinegar together and drizzle on salad.

AUSTRALIA

FUN FACTS ABOUT
FACT AUSTRALIA

Cuisine in Australia is a fusion of many different cuisines because of the many different cultures that have immigrated to the country —Asian, German, Italian and Lebanese, to name a few. The British settlers first arrived in 1788 and brought Western-style produce and farming practices to the continent.

BRAIN TEASERS

My name is "Balmain", I am a delicacy from the ocean, I taste like lobster, I also crawl and when I show up, so does the exterminator.

I am really cute, I am a marsupial, I am not very social, I am called a bear but do not belong to the bear family.

Answers:
Koala
Balmain Bug

CHEF REMMI TIP

Australia enjoys a huge variety of fruits and vegetables, including squash. I know it sounds weird to put squash in a salad, but it is so good. I also love pomegranate. Getting the seeds out is easier than you think. Get a big bowl of water, cut the pomegranate in half, submerge the pomegranate in the water and gently loosen the seeds. The seeds fall to the bottom and the membrane floats to the top. Just drain the water and you have a pile of sweet goodness!

Chef Remmi

My Recipe Notes

Entries
Entrées / Entradas   **Visas**   Departures
Sorties / Salidas

Age:

Date:

Where I cooked:

Entries
Entrées / Entradas   **Visas**   Departures
Sorties / Salidas

Who I cooked for/with:

This recipe is:

Other:

Cottage Pie

INGREDIENTS

POTATO TOPPING
2 lbs Yukon gold potatoes
   (unpeeled/medium dice/cooked)
½ c sour cream (fat free)
½ c chicken broth (fat free)
Salt and pepper to taste

PIE
2 T olive oil
½ c onions (small dice)
½ c celery(medium dice)
2 carrots (medium dice)
1 ½ lb lean ground beef
3/4 c beef broth
1 T tomato paste
1 c frozen peas
Salt and pepper to taste
3 T fresh parsley (sliced)

DIRECTIONS

Prepare potatoes as directed. Mash potatoes with the remaining ingredients and set aside. In medium pan, add the oil, onions, celery, carrots and meat. Cook on medium-low until meat is no longer pink. Drain any grease. Add remaining ingredients except the parsley and simmer until thickened. Place pie ingredients in the bottom of a medium casserole dish. Spread potato mixture over the pie. With the back of a medium spoon, sweep the potato up to form peaks. Bake in a preheated 350-degree oven for 20-30 minutes until warmed through. Remove from oven and garnish with parsley.

In this recipe I used onions, carrots and celery to flavor the dish. The combination of these 3 ingredients is called "mirepoix," which was created in France.

FUN FACTS ABOUT
FACT
AUSTRALIA

Even though Australia has one of the most varied cuisines in the world, it does not have a national dish, but one of their iconic dishes is meat pies.

"Carols by Candlelight" is a Christmas tradition where families with blankets and picnic baskets gather in every city the week before Christmas and sing Christmas carols while holding candles.

BRAIN TEASER

I am the national gemstone of Australia, I am mined, I am really valuable when I am black, I supply over 90% of the world's demand for this precious stone and I start with "O".

Answer:
Opal

CHEF REMMI TIP

Meat pies are eaten pretty frequently in Australia. I have made this pie a hundred times and always called it "Shepherd's Pie." After reading about Australia, I realized I had been making "Cottage Pie," because beef is the main ingredient. "Shepherd's Pie" is made with lamb or mutton. It makes sense, sheep –shepherd. Yeah!

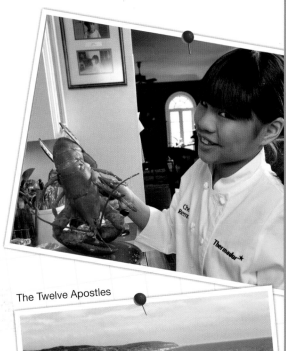

The Twelve Apostles

My Recipe Notes

Entries
Entrées / Entradas   Visas   Departures
Sorties / Salidas

Age:

Date:

Where I cooked:

Entries
Entrées / Entradas   Visas   Departures
Sorties / Salidas

Who I cooked for/with:

This recipe is:

Other:

Kiwi fruit Salad

INGREDIENTS

6 kiwi fruit (peeled/sliced ½")
1 ½ c strawberries (thick slices)
1 large banana (sliced ½")
2 T orange juice
1 t honey

DIRECTIONS

Prepare fruit as directed and place in medium bowl.
Mix orange juice with the honey and then toss onto
the salad.

Australia has 3 seasons
to grow strawberries.
That's heaven!

FUN FACTS ABOUT
FACT
AUSTRALIA

Perth is the origin of "Pavlova" (this is debated by New Zeelanders), a meringue dessert topped with fresh fruit and named after Anna Pavlova, a ballet dancer. It's a beautiful dish!

Kangaroos live all over Australia, and while we think they are totally cute, they are also a source of food for Australians and the 55 countries where the meat is exported. Check out "Kangaroo Tail Stew. "Yum? Perhaps! And yes, you can find a recipe for this.

🔍 BRAIN TEASER

I originated in Australia, I am a Smith, I am an apple and I am female, old and sweet.

Answers:
Granny Smith Apple

TIP

CHEF REMMI TIP

Fruit salads are often served as a dessert. Try any combination of 3 different fruits. Most Australians eat their fruit fresh and not cooked.

Remmi's own Italian dressing kit

Kangaroos

My Recipe Notes

Entries
Entrées / Entradas **Visas**
Departures
Sorties / Salidas

Age:

Date:

Where I cooked:

Entries
Entrées / Entradas **Visas**
Departures
Sorties / Salidas

Who I cooked for/with:

This recipe is:

Other:

46

SOUTH AMERICA

PERU

The birthplace of lima beans, the country of Peru is very food-centered. This South American country brings together the flavors of many of Peru's harvest foods: beans and potatoes, along with a little spice from south of the border.

CHEF REMMI SMITH

Map It
★ A4

GLOBAL COOKING

MENU

Potato Salad
Peruvian Stuffed Avocados
Beef and Rice Timbale
Grapes and Melon with Pineapple Sherbet

Potato Salad

INGREDIENTS

2 lbs Yukon gold potatoes (do not peel)
1 t olive oil
1/4 habanero chili
1 garlic clove
1/4 c milk (low fat)
8 oz cottage cheese(low fat)
2 Saltine crackers
Salt and pepper to taste
4 butter lettuce leaves
¼ c celery (sliced thin)
2 hard boiled eggs (sliced)
1 T fresh parsley

DIRECTIONS

Cook potatoes in water until tender. Sauté the chili pepper and garlic in oil until tender. In a blender, add the chili, garlic, milk, cottage cheese, crackers and salt and pepper. Blend ingredients. The consistency should be a very thick sauce. Place the lettuce leaves on a medium platter. Slice potatoes and place on lettuce. Sprinkle the potatoes with the celery. Spoon cheese mixture on top of potatoes. Garnish with eggs and parsley.

**This is a very popular Peruvian appetizer.
I know this dish sounds a bit weird,
but it is so delicious!**

PERU

BRAIN TEASERS

I originated from Peru, I am a bean and I am the capital.

I am the biggest cat in the Americas, and a car is named after me.

Answers:
Lima
Jaguar

FUN FACTS ABOUT

FACT

PERU

Peru is located on the 4th largest continent South America and has approximately 6% of the world's population.

Potatoes originated from Peru and are served with most meals. There are more than 3,000 different varieties cultivated.

Red chili peppers

CHEF REMMI TIP

Getting the right amount of heat from the chili pepper is the trick to the potato salad. These peppers are HOT! I know, as I experimented with many versions until I got it right. If you don't like heat, just omit the pepper. I couldn't ignore this dish – it must be on every Peruvian menu.

Peruvian cuisine is growing in popularity. There is a big selection of fresh ingredients and many of the dishes are a fusion of Spanish, African and Chinese influences.

My Recipe Notes

Entries
Entrées / Entradas **Visas** *Departures*
Sorties / Salidas

Age:

Date:

Where I cooked:

Entries
Entrées / Entradas **Visas** *Departures*
Sorties / Salidas

Who I cooked for/with:

This recipe is:

Other:

PERUVIAN
Stuffed Avocados

INGREDIENTS

2 avocados (sliced in half with seeds removed)
1 c tomato (medium dice)
1 c cucumber (medium dice)
1 ½ T sweet onion (sliced thin)
¼ c extra virgin olive oil
¼ c lime juice
2 T fresh cilantro leaves (sliced)
1 t honey
Salt and pepper to taste
2 T fresh parsley (sliced)

DIRECTIONS

Prepare ingredients as directed. In medium bowl, mix all the ingredients together, except for the avocados and parsley. Toss the salad with the dressing. Place the avocados on a platter. Fill the avocados with the salad and garnish with fresh parsley.

This is so easy to make, and it is a beautiful presentation. Remember, people eat with their eyes and not just their stomachs!

PERU

Machu Picchu

It is one of the things you get to do in the U.S. when you turn 18, but it is mandatory when you turn 18 in Peru and it is a very important decision.

If I were a boat I would be able to do this on water, people build their homes on me and I am a certain kind of island on Lake Titicaca.

Answers:
Vote
Floating

FUN FACTS ABOUT
FACT **PERU**

The avocado – one of the most wonderful flavors in the world – first cultivated in Peru.

Machu Picchu is one of the New Seven Wonders of the World and is located in Peru. This "City of Incas" was built in 1450 and is believed to be the estate of Emperor Pachacuti.

CHEF REMMI TIP

There are a ton of recipes for "Stuffed Avocado." What a cool way to serve this incredible treat. Try this one, but experiment with other recipes for avocado as well.

My Recipe Notes

Entries
Entrées / Entradas **Visas** Departures
Sorties / Salidas

Age:

Date:

Where I Cooked:

Entries
Entrées / Entradas **Visas** Departures
Sorties / Salidas

Who I Cooked For/With:

This recipe is:

Other:

Beef and Rice
TIMBALE

INGREDIENTS

2 c uncooked rice (Jasmine
  or Basmati are awesome!)
4 c water
1 c peas (frozen)
2 T olive oil (divided)
1 large sweet potato (peeled/
  medium dice/roasted)
2 garlic cloves (minced)
½ c onion (small dice)
1 lb ground beef

4 oz can Hatch chiles
14 oz can diced tomatoes
1 t paprika
1 t cumin
¼ c fresh parsley (sliced/
  divided)
Salt and pepper to taste
4 hard boiled eggs (sliced)
Cooking spray

DIRECTIONS

Prepare rice according to package instructions. Add frozen peas to the rice 5 minutes before the rice is finished cooking. Prepare sweet potato as directed and place on baking sheet. Drizzle 1 T of the olive oil on the potato and place in 400-degree oven for 15 minutes or until tender. In medium pan, sauté the onion and garlic in the remaining 1 T olive oil for 2 minutes. Add the ground beef and sauté until no longer pink. Drain any grease from the beef. Add chiles, tomatoes, paprika, cumin, 2 T parsley and sweet potato. Simmer for 10 minutes. Spray a 6 to 8 ounce bowl with cooking spray. Fill 1/3 of the bowl with rice followed by a layer of eggs, meat and then another layer of rice. Press the mixture firmly in the mold. Turn bowl upside down on serving plate. Prepare additional servings on separate plates. Garnish with the remaining 2 T parsley.

There were several Peruvian main dishes I experimented with, but when I tried this one, I knew it was the perfect recipe – kid friendly, delicious and so fun to make!

PERU

BRAIN TEASERS

I wear these on my feet to the beach, and I need to be exchanged between the Inca man and woman to be considered married.

Answer:
Sandals

FUN FACTS ABOUT

FACT PERU

The world has 32 different climates, and Peru has 28!

The largest river in the world, The Amazon, originates in Peru.

Cuy is a special Peruvian dish that is served on special occasions. What is it? A guinea pig, of course!

CHEF REMMI TIP

Many meals in Peru are served with a potato dish and a rice dish. Works for me!

Ok, I know the directions for the Beef and Rice Timbale are long, but it really isn't a complicated recipe at all. This dish is incredible.

The Amazon River

My Recipe Notes

Entries
Entrées / Entradas **Visas** *Departures*
Sorties / Salidas

Age:

Date:

Where I cooked:

Entries
Entrées / Entradas **Visas** *Departures*
Sorties / Salidas

Who I cooked for/with:

This recipe is:

other:

Grapes and Melon
WITH PINEAPPLE SHERBET

INGREDIENTS

1 c grapes (sliced in half)
2 c melon (medium dice)
4 scoops pineapple sherbet

DIRECTIONS

Prepare ingredients as directed.
Divide ingredients onto 4 small plates.

Enjoy!
It is a great
combination!

PERU

Remmi plays a game of Sapo with her friends

BRAIN TEASERS

I am a pretty cool creature - I love companionship. I am social, curious, gentle and I can hum, too! I can carry about 80 pounds on my back, and I work well in the mountains.

Answer: Llama

FUN FACTS ABOUT
FACT PERU

The "Chirimoya" is a local vegetable that tastes like strawberries (my favorite, you know) and cream. Yum! Can't wait to go to Peru someday and try this treat.

"Sapo" is a very popular coin toss game where a bronze frog sits on top of a box with holes in it. Getting the coin in the frogs mouth determines the winner, but it is tricky. You have to be able to throw the coin like a Frisbee.

CHEF REMMI TIP

Grapes, pepino melons and pineapples are all grown in Peru. Chances are you will not be able to find the pepino, so just go ahead and use a melon of your choice. Peru has some really unusual fruits that I have never heard of and would love to try!

Pepino melons

Chef Remmi hangs out with the llamas

My Recipe Notes

Entries
Entrées / Entradas   Visas   Departures
Sorties / Salidas

Age:

Date:

Where I cooked:

Entries
Entrées / Entradas   Visas   Departures
Sorties / Salidas

Who I cooked for/with:

This recipe is:

Other:

ASIA

LEBANON

Lebanon is located on the Eastern coast of the Mediterranean Sea. The sea has a big influence on Lebanese cuisine and adds to the lightness of the fare. Journey through my take on Lebanon cuisine with these delicious dishes!

Map It ★ E2

MENU

Tabouli
Lebanese Salad
Beef and Potato Sauté
Rice Pilaf
Lemon Yogurt

Tabouli

INGREDIENTS

½ c burghul (cracked wheat)
½ c water (boiling)
2 large tomatoes (small dice)
½ cucumber (peeled/small dice)
3 green onions (sliced ¼" on diagonal)
2 c flat leaf parsley (finely chopped)
1 ½ t dried mint
¼ t allspice
¼ c + 1 T lemon juice (fresh is better)
¼ c olive oil
½ t lemon zest
Salt and pepper to taste

DIRECTIONS

Prepare all ingredients as directed. In medium bowl, mix burghul and ½ c boiling water. Place a towel over top of bowl to keep the steam in. Let it cool. In medium bowl, mix all of the remaining ingredients. Test the burghul to make sure it is soft (if not, add a little water and microwave for 30 seconds). Add burghul when cool. Add equal amounts of lemon juice/olive oil if it is too dry.

YUM! YUM! YUM!

LEBANON

CHEF REMMI TIP

Pita is the number one food staple in Lebanon and is a part of every meal. You can buy them or there are recipes you can try and make yourself. Either way, be sure to toast them – crispy ones are awesome!

Fresh baked pita bread

FUN FACTS ABOUT
LEBANON

Lebanon is located on the largest continent, Asia.

The greeting between close friends is 3 kisses on the cheeks (alternating).

My Recipe Notes

Age:

Date:

Where I cooked:

Who I cooked for/with:

This recipe is:

Other:

BRAIN TEASER

I am the size of Lebanon, and I am the 3rd smallest state in the US.

Answer: Connecticut

72

Lebanese Salad

INGREDIENTS

SALAD
2 c Romaine lettuce (sliced 1" strips)
½ pint cherry tomatoes (sliced in half)
1 cucumber (peeled and sliced)
1 carrot (matchstick cut)
2 green onions (sliced)
3 T fresh parsley (sliced)

DRESSING
¼ c olive oil
¼ c lemon juice
¼ t lemon zest
1 ½ T dried mint
1 garlic clove (crushed)
Salt and pepper to taste

DIRECTIONS

Prepare salad ingredients as directed and place in medium bowl.
Mix dressing ingredients in a jar. Toss the salad with the dressing
just before serving.

This dish is great, because it is so simple and full of veggies!

Chef Remmi dances with friends

CHEF REMMI TIP

You can make a feast by serving all of these dishes – just add the pita and, for dessert, slice up some fruit, which is very popular. Examples of native fruits are melons, oranges, grapes and apricots.

FUN FACTS ABOUT
LEBANON

FACT

Lebanese cuisine is considered the finest in the Mediterranean, and it is healthy and always beautifully presented.

My Recipe Notes

Age:

Date:

Where I cooked:

Who I cooked for/with:

This recipe is:

Other:

The Pigeon Rocks of Beirut, Lebanon

Chef Remmi poaches an egg

 BRAIN TEASER

I am the oldest of its kind, I am so respected that when I get too old to be eaten I am kissed before being thrown away, I am part of every meal and, sometimes, I am used in place of a fork.

Answer:
Pita Bread

76

Beef and Potato Sauté

INGREDIENTS

3 c Yukon gold potatoes (do not peel/small dice)
1 lb ground beef (lean)
1/2 c onion (small dice)
¼ t allspice
1 c vegetable broth
1 c water (or more if needed)
¼ c fresh parsley + 2 T (for garnish)
Salt and pepper to taste
4 poached eggs (1 per serving)
  *see poaching directions below

DIRECTIONS

Prepare potatoes as directed and place in small bowl of water. In medium pan, sauté the meat and onions until meat is no longer pink. Drain off any grease. Drain the potatoes from the water. Add potatoes, allspice, ¼ c parsley, broth, and the water to the meat mixture. Cook on medium-low until the potatoes are tender. Add more water if necessary, just to cover the potatoes and allow them to cook. Add salt and pepper to taste. Place a serving of the beef and potato mixture on a plate and top with a poached egg. Sprinkle remaining parsley as a garnish.

TO PREPARE THE POACHED EGGS: Crack 4 eggs into small bowl. In medium pan, add 4 cups of water and 2 1/2 T of lemon juice and bring to a slow boil. Place eggs in the water and cook until the egg whites are cooked - 1 to 2 minutes. Remove eggs with a slotted spoon.

Lebanese cuisine serves up a lot of starches, and they are especially known for their love of potatoes. Potato dishes are usually prepared by the frying method. The dishes are served as appetizers and, as a main dish without meat. Red meat is not a big part of the cuisine, and if used in a recipe it is usually lamb. The potato dishes are very creative using different spices and adding vegetables. You can also make this dish without the eggs-but it adds a creamy sauce to the dish when the eggs are lightly poached. YUM-longtime family favorite!

LEBANON

CHEF REMMI TIP

You can make a meatless meal by only serving the rice with yogurt and one of the salad dishes. Make sure you serve with pita!

To make this a traditional Lebanese meal, prepare these recipes in appetizer (mezza) portions. But be prepared, you'll need to create at least another 25 dishes (mezzas) to make it an authentic Lebanese experience. That's right, the minimum is 30 different dishes!

FUN FACTS ABOUT
FACT ## LEBANON

Lebanese generosity and hospitality is extended through food (my favorite subject!) An unexpected visitor will always be invited to stay for a meal. Be sure to save room for seconds...this is good manners and shows the hostess that you are enjoying the food!

My Recipe Notes

Entries Entrées / Entradas	Visas	Departures Sorties / Salidas
Age:		
Date:		
Where I cooked:		

Entries Entrées / Entradas	Visas	Departures Sorties / Salidas
Who I cooked for/with:		
This recipe is:		
Other:		

🔍 BRAIN TEASERS

I was the first Olympic flame, and I am a sign of peace and goodwill.

I am the geometric shape of Lebanon.

Rice Pilaf

INGREDIENTS

1 T olive oil
2 c rice
¾ c capellini (broken in 2" pieces)
2 ¼ c water
2 c chicken broth (low sodium)
Salt and pepper to taste
¼ c almonds (toasted)

DIRECTIONS

In medium pan, heat the olive oil and then add the capellini. Sauté until the pasta is a golden color. Add the rice, water, chicken broth, salt and pepper. Bring to a boil and then turn the burner on low and put a lid on the pan. Cook for 20 minutes. Sauté almonds in small pan until golden and sprinkle on rice.

This dish is heavenly. It has both rice and pasta in it – two of my favorites!

LEBANON

Kafta and Kibbi

CHEF REMMI TIP

I have fallen in love with Lebanese foods and their cooking methods are very easy....so be sure to experiment with other recipes from this region. Try Kafta and Kibbi for sure.

FUN FACTS ABOUT
LEBANON

FACT

The Lebanese home always has a stock of yogurt, pickles, olives, nuts, fruits, herbs and spices.

The majority of the cultivated land is in olive and citrus groves.

My Recipe Notes

Entries
Entrées / Entradas **Visas** Departures
Sorties / Salidas

Age:

Date:

Where I cooked:

Entries
Entrées / Entradas **Visas** Departures
Sorties / Salidas

Who I cooked for/with:

This recipe is:

Other:

 **BRAIN TEASER**

Due to war, I was destroyed and rebuilt 7 times, and I am the largest city in Lebanon.

Answer:
Beirut

Lemon Yogurt

INGREDIENTS

2 c plain yogurt (nonfat)
1 ½ T lemon juice
1 t lemon zest
½ t coriander
Salt and pepper to taste

DIRECTIONS

Mix all ingredients in a bowl and serve with the rice pilaf.

I love this yogurt. Great citrus flavor!

LEBANON

CHEF REMMI TIP

If you love yogurt like I do, then you should try it with this rice dish – you will probably not eat any kind of rice dish any more without your yogurt. Spiced up or plain, homemade or from the container...I love it with rice.

FUN FACTS ABOUT
FACT LEBANON

Lebanese enjoy playing all kinds of board games...especially Monopoly!

Enjoying a meal is very social. Lebanese never eat alone.

My Recipe Notes

	Entries Entrées / Entradas	Visas	Departures Sorties / Salidas
Age:			
Date:			
Where I Cooked:			

	Entries Entrées / Entradas	Visas	Departures Sorties / Salidas
Who I Cooked For/With:			
This recipe is:			
Other:			

Traditional Lebanese cuisine

BRAIN TEASER

I am at the beginning of every meal and sometimes a lot of me are the meal.

Answer:
Mezza

EUROPE

ITALY

Nestled in the south of Europe, Italy has different flavors for its food from North to South. Join me as I bring together all the flavors in between with these easy and tasty dishes you'll be sure to love!

Map It
★ D2

MENU

White Bean Crostini
Butternut Risotto Bowls
Chicken Piccata with Spinach and Angel Hair Pasta
Italian Salad with Lemon Vinaigrette
Fresh Fruit and Cheese

White Bean Crostini

INGREDIENTS

1 can of Great Northern beans (rinsed and drained)
Zest of 1/2 lemon
Juice of 1 1/2 lemons
1 1/2 T fresh basil (chiffonade)
1 T olive oil
Salt and Pepper to taste
I baguette (½" slices/toasted)
Fresh parsley for garnish

DIRECTIONS

Prepare ingredients as directed. In a bowl, add all of the ingredients except the baguette and parsley. Fold the beans into the sauce mixture. Place crostini rounds on a platter and spoon a tablespoon of the mixture on each round. Garnish with parsley.

Crostini is often served with different ingredients,
like cheeses, meats and vegetables.
Try this one – it's yummy!

ITALY

Nuts and olive

 CHEF REMMI TIP

A formal Italian meal consists of eight different dishes being served. The only courses missing from my Italian menu are "Aperitivo," a light appetizer, like nuts and olives, "Contorno," vegetables, served separately but with the "Secondo" and "Dolce," which is usually a sweet dessert, like Tiramisu.

"Chiffonade" sounds fancy, but it is just an easy way to thinly slice herbs.

Tiramisu

My Recipe Notes

Entries
Entrées / Entradas   Visas   Departures
Sorties / Salidas

Age:

Date:

Where I cooked:

Entries
Entrées / Entradas   Visas   Departures
Sorties / Salidas

Who I cooked for/with:

This recipe is:

Other:

Italy is located on the continent of Europe, which is the 6th largest and contains 11% of the world's population.

Numerous inventions came from Italy: the piano, cello, violin, thermometer and typewriter, to name a few.

Violin

BRAIN TEASER

My story was created in Italy, and when I lie, my nose grows.

Answer:
Pinocchio

Butternut Risotto
BOWLS

INGREDIENTS

4 small butternut squash
3 T olive oil (divided)
7 c chicken stock
½ c sweet onion (small dice)
1 ½ c Arborio rice

Salt and pepper to taste
¼ c grated Parmesan cheese
2 T fresh sage leaves
¼ t fresh nutmeg

DIRECTIONS

The bottom half of each squash will be the "bowl" the risotto will be served in. Cut the tops of the squash off where the vegetable is wider. Scoop the seeds out of the squash bowls with a spoon. Place the squash bowls on a large baking sheet. Peel the tops of the squash and cut into medium size cubes. Place cubed squash on the baking pan with the squash bowls. Drizzle 2 T of the olive oil on the squash bowls and cubes. Add salt and pepper to taste. Bake the squash in a preheated 400 degree oven for 30 minutes or until the cubed squash is tender. Remove the cubed squash from the pan and set aside. Place the squash bowls back into the oven until they are tender. Place chicken stock in medium pan and bring to a simmer. In a separate medium pan, add the remaining oil and onions and sauté for 2 minutes. Add the rice to the pan and sauté for 4 to 5 minutes. Add 2 ladles of the chicken stock and stir every few minutes. When the mixture becomes dry add more stock and stir until the rice is cooked through and creamy. This should take 25 to 30 minutes. Stir in the cubed squash and Parmesan. Place each squash bowl on separate serving plates. Spoon risotto into the bowls and garnish with nutmeg and fresh sage leaves. Presenting the risotto in the squash bowls was inspired by Chef Antonio, who taught me the art of sautéing.

I know these directions seem long, but the hardest part of this recipe is being patient while the rice cooks. The wait is so worth it – creamy and dreamy! -Remmi

ITALY

TIP CHEF REMMI TIP

Researching Italy's cuisine was fascinating. There are 20 different regions and their cooking styles, regional foods and dishes are very different. It is interesting to explore and experiment with different foods.

Fresh-served Italian cuisine

My Recipe Notes

Entries Entrées / Entradas	Visas	Departures Sorties / Salidas
Age:		
Date:		
Where I cooked:		

Entries Entrées / Entradas	Visas	Departures Sorties / Salidas
Who I cooked for/with:		
This recipe is:		
Other:		

FUN FACTS ABOUT
ITALY

FACT

Marcella Polini Hazan, born in 1924 in the Italian seaside town of Cesenatico, wrote a cookbook, "The Classic Italian Cookbook", in 1973 that introduced classic Italian cuisine in America.

your text here
your text

Chef Remmi makes a pizza with friends

BRAIN TEASER

I was created in Naples, often I am delivered and in America I am consumed 350 times per second, making me a pretty popular dish.

Answer: Pizza

chicken Piccata
WITH SPINACH AND ANGEL HAIR PASTA

INGREDIENTS

½ lb angel hair pasta (cooked
  al dente)
2 chicken breasts (boneless/
  skinless/butterflied and cut in half)
½ c flour (reserve 2 t for sauce)
2 T olive oil
1 t garlic (minced)

1 c chicken broth (low sodium/
  fat free) (divided)
2 T lemon juice
1 T capers (drained)
1 lemon (sliced thin)
2 c baby spinach leaves
¼ c fresh Italian parsley (sliced)
Salt and pepper to taste

DIRECTIONS

Prepare all ingredients as directed. Place chicken in a plastic bag. Flatten
each chicken piece with a mallet* to ½" thickness. In medium sauté pan,
add the oil and garlic and sauté 1 minute. Sprinkle desired amount of salt
and pepper on each chicken cutlet and lightly dust with flour. Turn heat
to medium and add chicken and sauté for 3 minutes on each side until
golden. Remove from pan and place on plate. Wipe pan of any remaining
grease. Add ¾ c broth, lemon juice and capers to pan and bring to a slow
boil. Combine remaining 1/4 cup of broth with the reserved 2 t of flour.
Stir mixture into the sauce in the pan. Bring the heat down to simmer and
add the lemon slices. Cook 2 minutes or until slightly thickened. Divide
the pasta onto 4 serving plates. Top each portion of pasta with ½ c of
spinach. Place chicken cutlet on spinach and spoon sauce with lemon
slices on the chicken. Garnish with fresh parsley.

The heat from the sauce will wilt the spinach slightly to make
it crisp and tender. Angel hair pasta is one of my favorites and,
combined with this light and lemony sauce, is magnificent!

*See Chef Remmi Tip on the next page

ITALY

CHEF REMMI TIP

If you do not have a meat mallet to pound the chicken, no worries, just use a glass bottle to pound the meat.

Be sure to have an adult handle the cooking of the pasta. I am allowed to cook pretty much anything in the kitchen, but I am still not allowed to cook pasta.

Pasta with fresh tomatoes and basil

My Recipe Notes

Entries
Entrées / Entradas   Visas   Departures
Sorties / Salidas

Age:

Date:

Where I cooked:

Entries
Entrées / Entradas   Visas   Departures
Sorties / Salidas

Who I cooked for/with:

This recipe is:

Other:

FUN FACTS ABOUT ITALY

Kids love to play "Fruit-Eater Wolf." One player is the wolf and the rest of the players name themselves a kind of fruit. When the wolf calls out a fruit that has been selected, you better run! The wolf is going to chase you!

Remmi shops for strawberries

BRAIN TEASER

It took over 300 years to build me, I am one of the Wonders of the World and I have been leaning since I was built.

Answer: Leaning Tower of Pisa

Italian Salad
WITH LEMON VINAIGRETTE

INGREDIENTS

3 c Romaine lettuce (sliced)
2 c baby spinach
2 c frisée (cut to bite size)
½ cucumber (sliced thin)
1 small onion (sliced thin)
1 carrot (grated)
2 T fresh parsley (sliced)
¼ c extra virgin olive oil
2 T fresh lemon juice
½ t honey
Salt and pepper to taste

DIRECTIONS

Prepare all vegetable ingredients as directed. On a medium platter, layer the vegetables in the order they are listed. In a small bowl, mix the oil, lemon juice, honey, salt and pepper. When ready to serve, drizzle the dressing onto the salad (do not toss).

I am pretty much a salad snob as I judge all restaurants on their salads for freshness, taste and presentation. The Italians are known for their "una bells insalata mista," or their beautifully presented salads. It's just not that hard to make a salad beautiful when you have colorful vegetables!

ITALY

 TIP

CHEF REMMI TIP

The salad is always served after the "Secondo," not before or with it.

My Recipe Notes

Entries Entrées / Entradas	Visas	Departures Sorties / Salidas
Age:		
Date:		
Where I cooked:		

Entries Entrées / Entradas	Visas	Departures Sorties / Salidas
Who I cooked for/with:		
This recipe is:		
Other:		

FUN FACTS ABOUT ITALY

Old Italian families selected names for their children that had strong meanings like: Leonardo (Like a Lion), Vera (Truth), Benito (Blessed), and Natalia (Born on Christmas).

Remmi plays dress-up

 **BRAIN TEASER**

When I am sick I turn this color, when I am scared I turn this color, and when I am embarrassed I turn this color. I am also the colors of the Italian Flag.

Answer:
Green, White, Red

fresh fruit
WITH CHEESE

INGREDIENTS

Mango (peeled and sliced)
Grapes
Fresh figs
Parmesan Reggiano
Pomegranate

DIRECTIONS

On medium platter, arrange prepared fruits and cheese.

> You have probably realized what you are going to find in this book is fruit for dessert. The Italians serve it with cheese as a dessert. There is nothing better than in-season fresh fruit. Unless it is strawberries, in-season or out of season, they are still my top food!

ITALY

CHEF REMMI TIP

There is so much you can do with pasta, the combinations are endless. Try making a simple tomato sauce... so easy...so fast... and just plain delicious on any type of pasta.

Remmi with her fresh-bought bags of pasta

My Recipe Notes

Entries Entrées / Entradas	Visas	Departures Sorties / Salidas
Age:		
Date:		
Where I cooked:		

Entries Entrées / Entradas	Visas	Departures Sorties / Salidas
Who I cooked for/with:		
This recipe is:		
Other:		

FUN FACTS ABOUT ITALY

60% of the world's treasured art is in Italy, mostly in their 3,000 museums.

Italy's national dish is pasta, and each person will consume about 50 pounds per year.

The Colosseum in Rome, Italy

BRAIN TEASER

I am the capital of Italy, I am the largest city and Alfredo Sauce was created here.

Answer:
Rome

112

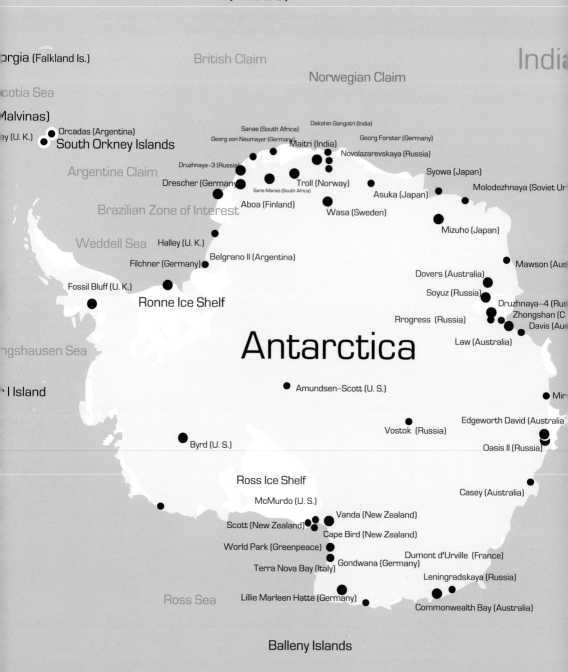

Atlantic Ocean

Bouvet Island (Norway)

South Sandwich Islands (Falkland Is.)

orgia (Falkland Is.)

British Claim

Norwegian Claim

India

cotia Sea

Malvinas)

ey (U. K.)   Orcadas (Argentina)
South Orkney Islands

Dakshin Gangotri (India)

Sanae (South Africa)   Georg Forster (Germany)
Georg von Neumayer (Germany)   Maitri (India)
Novolazarevskaya (Russia)

Syowa (Japan)

Argentine Claim

Druzhnaya-3 (Russia)
Drescher (Germany)   Troll (Norway)
Sarie Marais (South Africa)   Asuka (Japan)   Molodezhnaya (Soviet Ur

Brazilian Zone of Interest   Aboa (Finland)   Wasa (Sweden)

Mizuho (Japan)

Weddell Sea   Halley (U. K.)

Belgrano II (Argentina)

Dovers (Australia)   Mawson (Aus

Filchner (Germany)   Soyuz (Russia)   Druzhnaya-4 (Rus
Zhongshan (C

Fossil Bluff (U. K.)   Rrogress (Russia)   Davis (Au

Ronne Ice Shelf   Law (Australia)

ngshausen Sea

Antarctica

Amundsen-Scott (U. S.)   Mir

I Island   Edgeworth David (Australia

Vostok (Russia)

Byrd (U. S.)   Oasis II (Russia)

Ross Ice Shelf   Casey (Australia)

McMurdo (U. S.)

Vanda (New Zealand)

Scott (New Zealand)   Cape Bird (New Zealand)

World Park (Greenpeace)   Dumont d'Urville (France)

Terra Nova Bay (Italy)   Gondwana (Germany)

Leningradskaya (Russia)

Ross Sea   Lillie Marleen Hatte (Germany)

Commonwealth Bay (Australia)

Balleny Islands

South Pacific Ocean

115

Macquarie Island (Australia)
Campbell Island (New Zealand)

ANTARCTICA

WARM SOUPS AND FROZEN TREATS

Antarctica is the southernmost continent on Earth. Antarctica is mostly covered in ice, so these smoothies use one of the country's best assets. Antarctica may have one of the coldest climates on the planet, but we will warm things up with these great soup recipes!

CHEF REMMI SMITH

Map It
★ D7

GLOBAL COOKIN

MENU

Turkey Curry Soup
Pumpkin Soup
Creamy Potato Soup
Strawberry Granola Fruit Smoothie

Turkey Curry Soup

INGREDIENTS

2 T olive oil
1 onion (medium/sliced)
1 celery stalk (sliced ¼")
¼ c flour
4 c chicken broth (low sodium/low fat)
2 carrots (sliced ½")
2 c turkey (cooked/diced medium)
1 14 oz can diced tomatoes
2 t curry powder
1 apple (large/medium dice)
Salt and pepper to taste
¼ c fresh parsley

DIRECTIONS

Prepare ingredients as directed. In large pan, sauté onions and celery in the oil for 3 minutes. Add the flour and gradually add the chicken broth. Bring to a boil and then turn to simmer. Add carrots, turkey, tomatoes, curry powder, apple, salt and pepper. Simmer until the carrots are tender. Serve with parsley as a garnish.

Curry is one of those incredible spices that I just can't live without. This soup is hearty, easy to make, and the apples are just a nice surprise!

My Recipe Notes

Entries Entrées / Entradas	Visas	Departures Sorties / Salidas
Age:		
Date:		
Where I cooked:		

Entries Entrées / Entradas	Visas	Departures Sorties / Salidas
Who I cooked for/with:		
This recipe is:		
Other:		

CHEF REMMI TIP

Curry powder is really a mixture of spices, and every cook has their own recipe. The most common ingredient in all curries is turmeric, which gives the yellow color to the curry and the dish.

Curry and turmeric spices

FUN FACTS ABOUT ANTARCTICA

FACT

Antarctica is the 5th largest continent, has no native population, no cities and no government.

98% of Antarctica is covered in ice and has 90% of the world's ice and 70% of the earth's fresh water.

Glaciers and icebergs of Antarctica

🔍 BRAIN TEASER

I am the tallest of my species, I am very social, I slide across ice on my belly to preserve my energy, my dad takes care of me until I am born, I am the top ruler of an empire and I am a penguin.

Answer:
Emperor.

120

Pumpkin Soup

INGREDIENTS

2 T olive oil
1 medium onion (small dice)
2 15 oz cans of pumpkin purée (not pie mix)
2 ½ c chicken broth (low sodium)
1 c water
1/4 t nutmeg
1/2 t cinnamon
1 c milk (fat free)
½ c half and half (fat free)
Salt and pepper to taste
½ c plain yogurt (fat free)
Fresh parsley sprigs

DIRECTIONS

In large pan, heat the olive oil and sauté the onions until tender. Add the pumpkin, broth, water, nutmeg and cinnamon. Bring to a gentle boil and then simmer for 5 to 7 minutes. Stir in milk, half and half, salt and pepper. Serve in individual bowls with a spoonful of yogurt and garnish with parsley.

A bit of history: this soup originated in Haiti and was served at the first Independence Day, January 1, 1804, to the French. To this day, this soup is still served for this celebration day. I always think of that story when I make this creamy, scrumdiddlyumptious soup! -Remmi

My Recipe Notes

Entries
Entrées / Entradas **Visas** Departures
Sorties / Salidas

Age:

Date:

Where I cooked:

Entries
Entrées / Entradas **Visas** Departures
Sorties / Salidas

Who I cooked for/with:

This recipe is:

Other:

CHEF REMMI TIP

Pumpkin soup is so easy to make. There are a lot of creative pumpkin soup recipes where black beans, apples, cranberries, sweet potatoes and many other ingredients are part of the soup. So, try different combinations and create your own pumpkin soup recipe!

FUN FACTS ABOUT ANTARCTICA

The Antarctic Treaty has been signed by 48 countries, and the Treaty allows only scientific exploration on the continent.

The coldest temperature recorded was -129F.

Different species of penguins, seals, whales and dolphins are in Antarctica, and many of the scientists are there to study these animals.

 BRAIN TEASER

I am the color of the sky, I do this when I cry real hard, I am the biggest animal that has ever lived on the planet, my tongue weighs as much as a grown elephant and for my first year of life I gain 200 pounds per day.

Answer:
Blue Whale

Creamy Potato Soup

INGREDIENTS

2 T olive oil
2 garlic cloves (diced)
1 medium onion (small dice)
1 lb Italian sausage (low fat/
casings removed/1" chunks)
2 c water
3 c chicken broth (low sodium/
low fat)
4 medium potatoes (cut in
quarters) *see note below

1 ½ c fresh mushrooms
(medium size, sliced in half)
½ t crushed red pepper
2 c kale (sliced/bite size)
½ c half and half (nonfat)
Salt and pepper to taste
2 T fresh parsley (sliced)

DIRECTIONS

Prepare ingredients as directed. In medium pan, heat oil and sauté garlic, onion and sausage until sausage is no longer pink. Drain the mixture of any grease and wipe the pan clean. Add the mixture back in the pan and add water, broth, potatoes, mushrooms and red pepper. Bring to boil and then simmer until the potatoes are almost done (still firm). Add the kale and simmer until it is tender. Stir in the half and half, salt and pepper. To serve, place 2 or 3 potato slices in bowl and then ladle the broth with mushrooms over top and garnish with parsley.

Note: If using Idaho potatoes or potatoes with thick skins, either peel or partially peel the potatoes. This soup is really distinctive, because the potatoes are not chopped up. Don't be tempted to chop them; these potatoes are luscious, luscious, luscious!

My Recipe Notes

Entries
Entrées / Entradas **Visas** Departures
Sorties / Salidas

Age:

Date:

Where I cooked:

Entries
Entrées / Entradas **Visas** Departures
Sorties / Salidas

Who I cooked for/with:

This recipe is:

Other:

TIP

CHEF REMMI NOTE

A tradition at my house on Christmas Eve is to have 3 different soups simmering on the stove with a big stack of small bowls and a big platter of cheese, fruits and breads. Family comes in to town, and friends always stop by. These are some of my favorites I am sharing with you.

FUN FACTS ABOUT ANTARCTICA

There are roughly 50 permanent research stations and 20 summer-only research stations. These stations are staffed with researchers, scientists and support personnel.

The majority of the permanent stations are located on the Antarctic Peninsula, because it is the warmest area on the continent. Temperatures get above freezing, up to 20°F in summer.

A research station located in Antarctica

BRAIN TEASER

Monkeys love me and I wear it around my waist, and I am another name for the Antarctic Peninsula.

Answer:
Banana Belt

Strawberry Granola
FRUIT SMOOTHIE

INGREDIENTS

1 c ice cubes
1 c frozen strawberries
1 banana
6 oz plain yogurt (low or nonfat)
2/3 c milk (low fat)
5 T granola (divided)
1 t honey (optional)

DIRECTIONS

Place all ingredients in a blender, except for 2 T of the granola. Add the honey if sweeter taste is desired. Blend and then pour into tall glass. Garnish with the remaining 2 T of granola.

The best smoothie ever!

My Recipe Notes

Entries Entrées / Entradas	Visas	Departures Sorties / Salidas
Age:		
Date:		
Where I Cooked:		

Entries Entrées / Entradas	Visas	Departures Sorties / Salidas
Who I Cooked For/With:		
This recipe is:		
Other:		

CHEF REMMI TIP

You only need this recipe to make a great and healthy frozen smoothie. You can substitute any kind of frozen fruit: mango, blueberries, peaches and more. You can also use a combination of fruits. Don't leave out the banana! It is critical!

FUN FACTS ABOUT ANTARCTICA

FACT

Food is brought in by air or boat to feed the people. In summer there are 4,000 inhabitants, and in the winter there are approximately 1,000.

The chef is considered one of the most important staff personnel at the research stations. Because of the harsh and desolate environment, food is a big morale booster.

Leopard seal

BRAIN TEASERS

I use my watch for this, I am a zone and I do not exist in Antarctica.

I am in Antarctica, I am the opposite of North and I am a pole.

Answers:
Time Zone
South Pole

NORTH AMERICA

PUERTO RICO

Puerto Rican food is hot and spicy! These recipes bring together the ingredients and flavors of this territory of the United States. Located in the Caribbean, Puerto Rican food takes on a fresh and healthy feel.

MENU

Black Bean Soup

Coleslaw with Lime Vinaigrette

Arroz con Pollo

Fresh Tomato Salsa and Avocado Cream

Mango and Coconut Fruit Cocktail

CHEF REMMI SMITH

Map It

★ B3

GLOBAL COOKING

Black Bean Soup

INGREDIENTS

1 T olive oil
1 c onion (medium dice/divided)
¼ c celery (medium dice)
½ c red bell pepper (medium dice)
1t garlic (minced)
2 14.5 oz cans black beans (undrained)
½ t cumin

2 c chicken broth (nonfat/low sodium/divided)
2T fresh parsley
1T jalapeño (seeded/minced)
Salt and pepper to taste
½ c yogurt (plain/nonfat)
1 avocado (firm/large dice)
½ c cilantro leaves

DIRECTIONS

In medium saucepan, heat the oil and then sauté 3/4 c onion, celery, bell pepper and garlic for 1 to 2 minutes. Add beans, cumin, 1c chicken broth, parsley, jalapeño, salt and pepper to taste. Bring to boil then turn down heat to simmer for 15 minutes. Add more of the remaining chicken broth for desired consistency. Serve soup with the remaining onion, yogurt, avocado and cilantro as sides.

Using canned beans, this soup is so easy to make! It's good..but when you have the time, making this soup with dried beans is supreme!

FUN FACTS ABOUT
PUERTO RICO
(FACT)

Puerto Rico is located on the third largest continent of North America and is the only continent that has every kind of climate.

 ## CHEF REMMI TIP

Most Puerto Rican meals start with a soup, and this is a popular one. You can get really creative with this one by adding different ingredients, like carrots or tomatoes. Often times it is puréed, but I like the texture of the beans. Reduce the chicken broth to ½ c and serve over angel hair pasta or rice for a great vegetarian meal. Don't skimp on the garnishes. They make the dish beautiful and special.

Caribbean Sea

My Recipe Notes

	Entries Entrées / Entradas	Visas	Departures Sorties / Salidas
Age:			
Date:			
Where I cooked:			

	Entries Entrées / Entradas	Visas	Departures Sorties / Salidas
Who I cooked for/with:			
This recipe is:			
Other:			

 # BRAIN TEASER

I am the largest of my species and can weigh as much as
2,000 pounds, I like the open ocean, I love jelly fish, when
I am born I have to find my way to the ocean without my
mom or dad, I am a turtle, you can make shoes out of my
hide and I am the opposite of front.

Answer:
Leatherback

coleslaw
WITH LIME VINAIGRETTE

INGREDIENTS

8 c green cabbage (sliced thin)
1 apple (medium dice)
¼ c green onion (sliced on diagonal)
1 jalapeño pepper (small/seeds
    removed/minced)
3T cilantro (sliced)
2T parsley (sliced)
3 T light oil (safflower/canola)
3T lime juice
2 t honey
Salt and pepper to taste

DIRECTIONS

Prepare ingredients as directed. In medium bowl,
add cabbage, apple, green onion, jalapeño pepper,
cilantro and parsley. In separate bowl, mix oil, lime
juice, honey, salt and pepper. Toss the coleslaw with
the dressing just before serving.

This crunchy coleslaw is
a little bit sweet and
a little bit spicy - the
best of both worlds!

PUERTO RICO

PUERTO RICO

FUN FACTS ABOUT
PUERTO RICO

FACT

The country is a commonwealth of the U.S. The people are citizens of the U.S., but they do not have the right to vote for the U.S. President.

CHEF REMMI TIP

Two popular dishes I didn't include are empanadas, which are little fried meat and vegetable pies, and plantain. There is a lot of frying going on in this cuisine, but look for alternative recipes that bake these. Both are real treats!

Empanadas

My Recipe Notes

Entries
Entrées / Entradas   **Visas**   Departures
Sorties / Salidas

Age:

Date:

Where I cooked:

Entries
Entrées / Entradas   **Visas**   Departures
Sorties / Salidas

Who I cooked for/with:

This recipe is:

Other:

The Puerto Rican flag

 **BRAIN TEASER**

Even though I am part of the U.S.,
I have my own organization and I
compete internationally.

Answer:
Olympic Team

144

Arroz Con Pollo

INGREDIENTS

1 chicken fryer
  (cut into 10 pieces,
  breast to be cut in half)
  and skin removed)
1 t paprika
Salt and pepper
1 ½ T olive oil (divided)
1 onion (large/small dice)
1 c each, red and green bell
  pepper (medium dice)

1 jalapeño pepper (medium/small dice)
2 garlic cloves (minced)
2 cups rice (jasmine or basmati)
3 ¼ c chicken broth (low sodium)
1 large tomato (medium dice)
½ t turmeric
Salt and pepper to taste
¾ c frozen peas
¼ c flat leaf parsley (sliced)
1 lime (sliced in wedges)

DIRECTIONS

Prepare ingredients as directed. Wash and pat the chicken dry. Season the chicken pieces with the salt, pepper and paprika. In a large pan heat 1 T of olive oil and add the chicken and sauté until golden brown on both sides. When chicken is done, remove from pan and set aside. Drain any grease from the pan. Add the remaining olive oil with the onions, peppers and garlic. Sauté for 1 to 2 minutes. Add the rice to the mixture and sauté for 1 to 2 minutes. Add the chicken broth, tomato, turmeric, salt and pepper. Bring to boil, place lid on pan and turn heat to low. Simmer for 15 minutes. Take lid off pan and add the peas on top of the rice and then the chicken. Place lid back on pan for 10-15 minutes until rice and chicken are fully cooked. After dish is fully cooked, remove chicken from pan. Fluff the rice and add the parsley. Place a mound of rice on individual plates and serve with 1 or 2 pieces of chicken and with the salsa and avocado cream and lime wedges.

This meal is good even without the salsa and cream, but it is unbelievably delicious with them!

FUN FACTS ABOUT
FACT
PUERTO RICO

The "Casa Blanca" mansion was built in 1592 by Ponce De León. His family and descendants lived there for 250 years. It is the oldest residence in the Western Hemisphere that has been continuously occupied.

The Casa Blanca mansion

CHEF REMMI TIP

Chicken is one of the favorite meats and Arroz Con Pollo is one of the most popular dishes served. While it takes a few steps to make, we are looking at only one pot to clean! It is also a very economical dish to make.

My Recipe Notes

	Entries Entrées / Entradas	Visas	Departures Sorties / Salidas
Age:			
Date:			
Where I cooked:			

	Entries Entrées / Entradas	Visas	Departures Sorties / Salidas
Who I cooked for/with:			
This recipe is:			
Other:			

Remmi shows some love for avocados

Palm trees of Puerto Rico

 BRAIN TEASER

I am in the mountains of Puerto Rico, there is more of me there than in all of the U.S. and I am between a penny and a dime.

Answer:
Nickel

148

Fresh Tomato Salsa AND Avocado Cream

INGREDIENTS

SALSA
2 c fresh tomatoes (medium dice)
¼ c onions (medium dice)
1t garlic (minced)
½ c cilantro leaves
1 jalapeño (seeded/diced small)
1 T lime juice
1 t olive oil
Salt and pepper to taste

AVOCADO CREAM
1 avocado (ripe/seeded/removed
  from skin)
½ c sour cream (nonfat)
1 T lime juice
Salt and pepper to taste

DIRECTIONS

SALSA
Prepare ingredients as directed. In small bowl, mix all ingredients together.

AVOCADO CREAM
In small bowl, lightly mash the avocado. In a separate bowl, combine the sour cream, lime juice, salt and pepper. Fold mashed avocado into the cream mixture.

I am totally into adding garnishes to dishes I make. More often than not, my garnishes are in the form of "salsas." Since the ingredients are usually fruits and vegetables...they are full of color and they add not only flavor but beauty to the dish. It's all about adding something special! -Remmi

FUN FACTS ABOUT
FACT
PUERTO RICO

El Yunque is the only U.S. tropical rainforest.

Puerto Rico has the largest single-dish radio telescope in the world. The dish covers 20 acres of land.

CHEF REMMI TIP

I added salsa and the avocado cream to the main entrée as sides. They are not necessary, but they do upgrade the dish to exceptional! If time is an issue, just make one of them!

151

My Recipe Notes

Age:

Date:

Where I cooked:

Who I cooked for/with:

This recipe is:

Other:

Rainforest of Puerto Rico

🗒️ TIP BRAIN TEASER

I am a dance that was created by Puerto Ricans that is popular all over the world, I am mostly made with tomatoes as an ingredient and I am usually eaten with chips.

Answer:
Salsa

Mango And Coconut
FRUIT COCKTAIL

INGREDIENTS

3 c mango (large dice)
2 c pineapple (large dice)
¼ c dried cherries
1/4 c fresh coconut
Nutmeg

DIRECTIONS

Prepare ingredients as directed. In a medium bowl, mix the mango, pineapple and dried cherries. Serve in individual bowls and sprinkle each with the coconut and just a tiny dash of nutmeg.

It is not too hard to find fresh coconuts in stores and fresh tastes the best!

FUN FACTS ABOUT PUERTO RICO

FACT

Puerto Rican children get to have 2 Christmases with presents which are Christmas Day and January 6th (Epiphany). On January 5th, children put grass, water and grains under their beds to feed the camels of the traveling Three Wise Men. The children wake up to presents under their bed left by the Wise Men.

CHEF REMMI TIP

Coconuts are popular as an ingredient in Puerto Rican foods. Look up on the internet how to open it – not the easiest!

Remmi shops for pineapples

My Recipe Notes

Entries Entrées / Entradas	Visas	Departures Sorties / Salidas
Age:		
Date:		
Where I cooked:		

Entries Entrées / Entradas	Visas	Departures Sorties / Salidas
Who I cooked for/with:		
This recipe is:		
Other:		

Coconut

🗒️ BRAIN TEASER

I am the oldest city in the U.S., I am a capital, I was founded by Ponce de León and if you eliminate the same letter in "sand" and "wand," that is who I am.

Answer:
San Juan

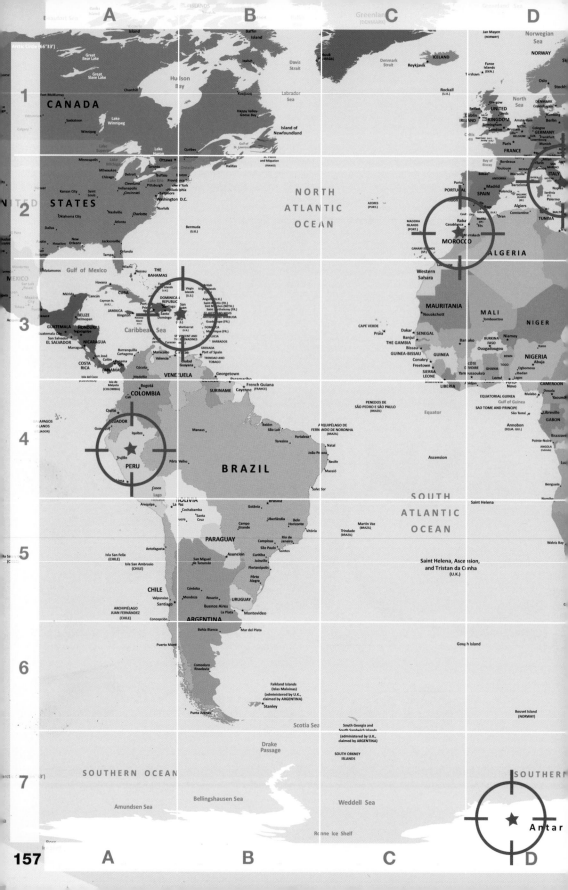

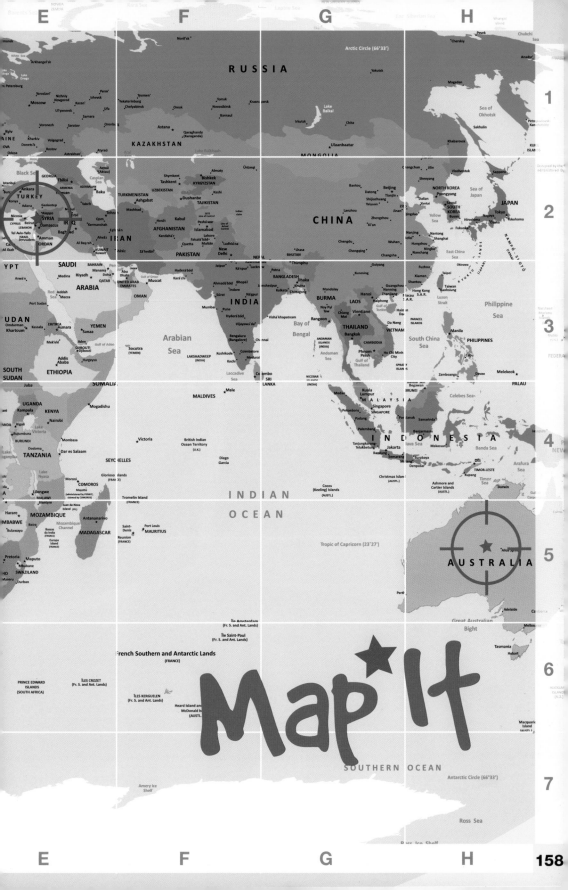